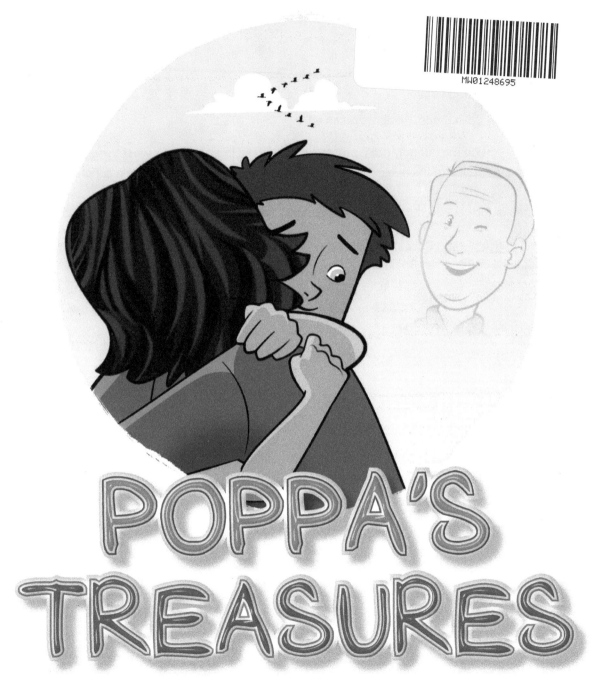

POPPA'S TREASURES

By J. A. Smith

Illustrations by Chad J. Thompson.

Printed in the United States of America

First Printing, 2023

ISBN 978-1-955791-80-9

Library of Congress Control Number: 2023919442

Ordering Information: Special discounts are available on quantity purchases by bookstores, corporations, associations, and others. For details, contact the publisher at sales@braughlerbooks.com or at 937-58-BOOKS.

For questions or comments about this book, please write to info@braughlerbooks.com.

Braughler™
Books
braughlerbooks.com

Dedication

For my mother whose treasure continues to fill my heart

The meaning of life is to find your gift.

The purpose of life is to give it away.

– Joy J. Golliver

POPPA'S TREASURES

By J. A. Smith

This Saturday is way different and it feels so odd. It used to be my favorite day of the week. As far back as I can remember, I spent every Saturday with Poppa. This is our very first Saturday without him. My dad always called his dad, "Poppa," so that was what the rest of the family called him too. Mom says even though Poppa is no longer with us he will always be in our hearts. I don't understand how that works.

I'm just lying here on my bed in my room, all by myself, tossing my baseball up in the air and catching it over and over. There's a knock on the door and Mom pops her head in.

"Hey Bub, we're going to do something special today. Up and at 'em!"

I give Mom the same look I give the teacher when she catches me daydreaming in class.

"Huh?" Then I ask," What could possibly be special today? I really don't feel like doing anything!"

"I know, but trust me. Dad and Sis are going too."

"Where?

"We're going on a treasure hunt."

"Mom," I say even more disappointed. "I'm past believing in pirate treasures."

"Oh, I know that. This has nothing to do with pirates. It's a really special kind of treasure hunting. Put your glove and ball down. C'mon, let's go."

Mom waits for me and follows me out the door. When we get outside, my sister is already in the backseat of the car, buckled in but looking as confused as me. Dad is in the front, behind the wheel. He doesn't look excited to me but he manages a smile when I get in the back with my sister. Mom gets in front with Dad, buckles in, and then asks,

"Are we all ready for our big adventure?"

When none of us answer, she doesn't seem to lose her excitement. She winks at Dad and then says,

"Treasure hunting here we come!"

It's not very far into our drive before I notice that Dad is taking all the same roads that we would take to go to Poppa's. I feel too sad to say anything. I know Poppa no longer lives there. Why would we be going to his house?

I start thinking about all the other Saturdays spent at Poppa's house. Sometimes we would play games or watch baseball on TV after doing some errands around the house. Poppa knew all

5

there was to know about baseball. Every now and then, he would get so excited or maybe a little angry at a call that he would say a cuss word. He would wink and I knew it would be our little secret. Of course, I wouldn't tell anybody. And I never repeated what he said.

Soon, I know it. We're at Poppa's street and then Dad turns onto it. He parks the car on the street, directly across from Poppa's house. There are so many people walking around outside his house that I can't believe my eyes. I still don't understand. Dad and Mom get out of the car. My sister and I don't move. We wait for

some kind of explanation. Then, Mom opens our door, peers in, and explains.

"Guys, as you know, Poppa no longer lives here and, unfortunately, we can no longer keep his house. We will need to sell it but before we do, we need to find and keep the treasures that Poppa and Nonna left for us.

"Poppa left us trunks of treasures?" my sister asks excitedly.

"Not exactly, Sis. He did indeed leave us treasures but these are way different from pirate trunks of treasures. These are extra special things that Poppa or Nonna left for you only, that you will love and want to keep like a precious treasure. I can't tell you what it will be. I am absolutely sure that you will know it when you find it. Walk all around the house, porch, garage, attic, and basement. Take your time. When you're done, we'll all meet back at the car. Now, go! Happy hunting!"

Dad gives us a big smile, grabs Mom's hand, and heads towards Poppa's house. My sister and I barely move away from the car and just watch for a while.

"There are so many people here. How can there be enough treasures for everybody?" she whines.

"You've got a good point," I add. "I'm not at all sure about this. I don't even like being here without Poppa."

Suddenly, I hear someone whistling. I turn and see Uncle Chaz. He's walking away from the garage swinging one of Poppa's tool boxes. Can a tool box be a treasure? I grab my sister's hand and start walking, still wondering about that tool box. I can't decide if I should go to the house first or the garage. Distracted, I bump into Aunt

Lee carrying two large plastic bags full of fabric scraps. Whenever we needed scissors, Poppa would send us up to Nonna's old sewing room so I know those bags came from there. My sister leaves to help her. Then I head to the house.

I feel a little more confident as I walk towards the house until I notice the porch looks different. All the wooden furniture is gone. When I enter the house, I see Uncle Wally sitting in Poppa's recliner; he's smiling but his eyes are closed and his hands are moving slowly up and down on the arms of the chair.

I go into the kitchen and find Aunt Rena tracing her hand over a recipe from a big folder of recipes. Tears fall down her cheek but she doesn't look sad. She looks so peaceful, I back out of the kitchen and return to the living room.

In the corner, Uncle Lou and my cousin Tony sit with several photo albums surrounding them. They have one open, pointing to something, laughing and laughing.

I walk into the dining room. I see my oldest cousin holding candlesticks that have been on the dining room table forever. Poppa once said that he's had them ever since he and Nonna got married. There is something about the way my cousin is holding them; you would think she's cuddling a baby!

As I watch, each person finds the treasure Poppa or Nonna specifically left for them. I know it's their own treasure because I can see their tears, laughter and smiles when they are holding it. It's like there's a voice in their hearts telling them what that special treasure will be. Finally, I understand what Mom said about Poppa always being in our hearts even if he can't be with us. I know that he really must have left a treasure just for me, too. Now, I need to find it.

I go outside to the porch, sit on the steps, and think about my favorite memories with Poppa. Saturdays, when the weather was perfect, Poppa used to drive to our house and pick up anyone who wanted to go fishing with

him. Not everyone liked to fish as much as me but sometimes Sis, Mom, Dad, or even some of my cousins would go with us. Poppa was happiest anytime fishing with family. He always picked out our poles, packed our lunches, snacks and drinks. When we got to one of his favorite spots, he would help us bait our hooks, set lines, and reel in our fish. He was in charge, loving every minute, but he made us feel so special while doing it. Then I smile knowing exactly what Poppa left just for me. I run to the garage, passing my cousin Ty coming out of it with

Poppa's tackle box. I see his joy but I also start to panic that my treasure may already be gone.

Once inside, I look towards the back wall. There, stored in the rack with two other poles, is no ordinary fishing pole. This is the pole with an open reel that Poppa was teaching me how to cast. He said that when I could do it all on my own, it was going to be my very own to keep. As I grab it from the rack, I hear Poppa's instructions. I know in my heart that I will now always hear his instructions when I'm using this very pole that he chose just for me. He may no longer be by my side but my heart

will let me hear his voice and feel his love and joy whenever "we" go fishing. I found my very own treasure and I cannot wait to share my excitement with Mom, Dad, and my sister. I rush to the car, carrying the pole but being very careful not to fall and break it.

It seems as if I'm at the car for hours before I see my sister walking toward me with a blanket that Poppa always said was extra special because it was handmade with Nonna's love. With the biggest smile, she says,

"Look at my treasure! I always loved this blanket because of the flowers on it and how

cozy it made me feel when we used to watch movies with Poppa."

I give her high fives and show her the pole.

"The last time I went fishing with Poppa, he told me that when I could cast with its reel without getting any tangles, this pole was going to have my name on it! This is the best treasure hunting ever!"

Sis gives me thumbs up. Neither of us can wait to share our excitement with Mom and Dad.

A few minutes later, Dad is walking towards the trunk of the car, carrying a big box. We meet him halfway there and show him our treasures.

"Wow," he says."I think those are the exact treasures Poppa and Nonna would have wanted you to have. Hey, look at my treasure!" he says holding out the box.

My sister and I look inside; it's full of hand carved ornaments that Poppa always put out at Christmas time. We jumped, hugged, and slapped hands. Finally, Mom arrives. She looks so happy seeing us celebrate.

"Well, well, well, "she says. "It looks to me that you got the hang of this treasure hunting. Poppa would love what you've found. I knew you would enjoy this day."

Then I notice that she isn't carrying anything. I wonder if her treasure is so small that it's in her pocket.

"Mom," I ask, "where's your treasure?"

"Oh, Bub," she says, "Poppa's treasure is and always has been with me. Every time I look into your eyes, I also see his."

Then she gives me the biggest hug ever!

Acknowledgements

Four simple words, "I believe in you," can indeed move mountains and make dreams a reality but no man is an island, and neither am I. From the inception of the story to its final copy, I've been fortunate to enlist the help of professionals, friends and family whose critiques guided and encouraged me. I am indebted to Braughler Books for patience and guidance, to Laura for helping me keep true to Bub's voice, to J.E. Irvin for sharing her expertise with syntax and editing, and to Les for teaching me how to picture my words. I am also so fortunate for my husband who always sees and hears two sides to every story, thereby giving voice to Poppa as well as Bub.

Printed in the USA
CPSIA information can be obtained
at www.ICGtesting.com
LVHW060717010224
770457LV00011B/55